# THE NEED TO KNOW LIBRARY

# EVERYTHING YOU NEED TO KNOW ABOUT

# RACISM

## ANGIE TIMMONS

Rosen
**YA**

New York

Published in 2018 by The Rosen Publishing Group, Inc.
29 East 21st Street, New York, NY 10010

**Library of Congress Cataloging-in-Publication Data**

Names: Timmons, Angie, author.
Title: Everything you need to know about racism / Angie Timmons.
Description: New York : Rosen Publishing, 2018. I Series: The
need to know library I Includes bibliographical references and
index. I Audience: Grades 7–12.
Identifiers: LCCN 2017019695I ISBN 9781508176763 (library bound)
IISBN 9781508176756 (pbk.) I ISBN 9781508176787 (6 pack)
Subjects: LCSH: Racism—History—Juvenile literature. I Race
relations—History—Juvenile literature.
Classification: LCC HT1507 .T56 2018 I DDC 305.8009—dc23
LC record available at https://lccn.loc.gov/2017019695

*Manufactured in the United States of America*

# CONTENTS

# INTRODUCTION

On the evening of June 17, 2015, twelve members of the Emanuel African Methodist Episcopal Church bible study group welcomed a newcomer, twenty-one-year-old Dylann Roof. The group—all Methodist African Americans at the historically black church in Charleston, South Carolina—did not care that Roof was white; the church welcomes all. Roof sat next to Clementa C. Pinckney, the pastor and a South Carolina state senator.

After listening for an hour and joining in a closing prayer, Roof stood up and began shooting.

He killed eight people within six minutes, shouting racial epithets as he fired.

A ninth victim later died at a hospital.

Only two women and a five-year-old girl survived the massacre of what the media soon began calling the Charleston Nine.

Roof was arrested in North Carolina the following morning. He faced multiple charges and life sentences in prison. In statements, he made one thing clear: he wanted to start a race war with the church shooting. The church—founded in 1816, central to the history of American slaves and civil rights, and in the heart of the old Confederacy—was a perfectly symbolic place to incite such a conflict.

Roof's attack happened at a time when race relations in the United States were already suffer-

The historically black Emanuel African Methodist Episcopal Church in Charleston, South Carolina, is where a self-proclaimed white supremacist murdered nine black people in 2015.

ing, mostly owing to high-profile instances of police brutality toward African Americans. In 2012, a neighborhood watch member named George Zimmerman was acquitted after fatally shooting an unarmed black teenager named Trayvon Martin in Florida. After his acquittal, the Black Lives Matter movement arose, aimed at stopping violence toward black people. The movement gained momentum and support, but unrest between law enforcement and African Americans didn't stop. In April 2015, a twenty-five-year-old black man in Baltimore, Freddie Gray, sustained injuries during an arrest that led to his death. Only one police officer faced charges for the incident. Those charges were dropped, and none of the other officers involved faced charges. Baltimore erupted in protest.

In his manifesto, Roof cited the Martin-Zimmerman incident as a turning point in his life. Angered by public outcry over these incidents, Roof became a white supremacist as he grew from teenager to adult. He radicalized his beliefs online, where he found others with extreme views on race relations.

The internet has given modern-day racists an avenue to pursue their dangerous beliefs by associating with like-minded individuals online. The rise of "alternative" media sites run by far-right, radical thinkers gives racists validation for their beliefs. Emboldened by these factors, hate groups have blossomed throughout the last few decades.

Despite the prevalence of racism and the new social delivery systems racists have to spread their message, not all is lost. By understanding racism and what drives it, people of all races can combat the problem by identifying and removing racism from private and public institutions—such as churches, governing bodies, and schools— and their communities. Education about other races can drive integration and celebrate diversity.

As global citizens, informed and compassionate dialogue between diverse individuals and groups must happen; otherwise, unnecessary tragedies will continue to happen.

# CHAPTER ONE

# RACISM EXPLAINED

More than 150 years after the Civil War, how can relations between white people and black people still be so strained?

The answer is complex. Racism in America has been addressed for many decades, spanning many generations. Civil disobedience, legal battles, and even violent conflicts such as the Civil War and some instances during the civil rights movements of the 1960s bookmark a turbulent history of race in this country. Though our society has progressed past the days of slavery and segregation, race relations obviously still need some work.

In this fast-paced and often turbulent world, defining racism is the first step in identifying and combating bias and prejudice based on a person's skin color or ethnicity.

## RACISM: AN EXCUSE FOR OPPRESSION

In its most basic definition, racism is any attitude or behavior that demonstrates the idea of superiority

Marchers protest segregation in Southern stores outside the F. W. Woolworth store in New York City in April 1960.

based solely on race. Racism is often accompanied by prejudicial or discriminatory practices based on racial superiority. Though experts like anthropologists and biologists have found no evidence that any race is superior to others, skin color and ethnicity have long been at the heart of conflicts almost as old as human-kind. For thousands of years, racism has been used as an excuse to oppress, enslave, and, in extreme cases, exterminate entire groups of people based solely on their skin color or ethnicity.

Documented accounts of racist statements and activities began with European colonization in the

# WHO IS A RACIST?

Racism takes many forms, and so do racists. In the United States, racism is most commonly associated with white attitudes and biases against African Americans. And while the history of racism in America does revolve largely around white-black race relations, not all racists are white, and not all victims of racism are black. For example, Americans of all colors adopted fearful attitudes regarding Muslims after the terrorist attacks of September 11, 2001. Ethnic and religious groups outside of Islam and predominantly Muslim countries can attest that Americans' post-September 11 fears are acutely active. Since the September 11 attacks, dozens of Sikhs—a predominantly Indian religion in which males wear turbans—have been attacked, killed, or victimized by arson or other violent crimes perpetrated by individuals or groups that targeted them because they wear turbans. Muslims and those mistaken for Muslims have been targeted by angry and fearful Americans since 2001—even though nearly all the victims had absolutely nothing to do with September 11.

Some racists develop if they feel marginalized by misfortune or economic downturn. For example, some Americans maintain a prejudice against Latin and South Americans who come across the American border to escape hostilities and corruption in their home countries because they believe these immigrants are stealing jobs from American citizens. In fact, many presidential and other political candidates have adopted this prejudice in their campaigns, promising to stem the flow

*(continued on the next page)*

*(continued from the previous page)*

of immigrants into America and returning jobs to citizens—despite overwhelming evidence that very few jobs performed by immigrants are jobs the average American citizen wants.

Racists can be any color, ethnicity, nationality, or religion. Because racism is based on misinformed ideas about and fear of difference, and socialized from generation to generation, racists are found in just about every level of society, age group, and corner of the world.

1600s. European countries with predominantly white populations launched exploration and colonization efforts in places like the New World (the Americas), Asia, and Africa. European explorers and colonists forced natives to submit. In many cases, this involved enslavement or forced removal of natives from their ancestral homelands, as was the case for many Native American tribes in the United States.

To understand European attitudes and actions toward nonwhites in the ages of exploration and colonization, scholars and historians have noted how Europeans viewed humanity overall as they began exploring outside their continent. Using sea vessels and weaponry more advanced and powerful than anything the native cultures they encountered had ever seen, Europeans began to view the natives of foreign continents as lesser beings. As European nations used their military and industrial might to force natives to submission, the assumption was that this submission was possible because the natives were inferior, their cultures savage. Even priests promoted the concept of

A marker in Conway, Arkansas, memorializes Cherokees forced from their native lands by white settlers in what history has come to call the Trail of Tears.

white superiority; European Christian nations engaged in holy wars against primarily nonwhite countries, operating under the notion that they had a responsibility to convert non-Christians in parts of Africa, Asia, and the Middle East to Christianity. These holy wars resulted in loss of life on both sides, but also the enslavement of nonwhite people from non-Christian nations. The Christian faith associates purity with the color white; Christians who encountered natives in foreign lands may have viewed their darker skin color as a negative sign, associated with evil. As white Europeans reached farther and farther around the globe, they used the ideas of Christianity and white superiority to justify claiming land in far-away nations and enslaving the inhabitants of nonwhite cultures.

## RACISM AND SOCIAL SCIENCE

As European countries steadily occupied more and more distant lands and coerced or enslaved natives, ill-informed facts and research regarding white superiority provided justification for oppression of nonwhites in the eighteenth and nineteenth centuries. Arthur de Gobineau, a nineteenth-century French diplomat and writer, was a strong proponent of racism. In his *Essay on the Inequality of Human Races*, Gobineau proposed that whites mixing with people of color dilutes the inherent superiority of the white race and threatens civilization. As a writer and diplomat, Gobineau did not have any credible science to back up his claims; however, this did not stop his contemporaries and future despots such as Adolf Hitler from adopting his theories to justify their oppressive actions.

In his 1859 book *On the Origin of Species*, Charles Darwin's theories were twisted by racists to justify a scientific basis for continued oppression of nonwhites. Darwin said species evolve and survive by adaptation and selection; weak species die out, and strong species prevail. Countries involved in colonization and enslavement of nonwhites seized the opportunity to use Darwin's theory for their own means, arguing whites were a stronger species and inherently superior to nonwhites. This served the interests of European imperialism in Africa and Asia and of Americans who enslaved and oppressed racial minorities. The fact that people of all races fall into one species—human—was ignored by powerful people from powerful countries to protect their interests and wealth.

In 1883, British mathematician Francis Galton created the science of eugenics, which promoted the idea that superior races would be able to prevail over inferior ones. Between the 1890s and 1940s, eugenicists posited that Jews, people of color, and homosexuals—among other groups—were inferior to heterosexual, Protestant white men from northern Europe. Hitler used Galton's theory to justify his extermination of Jews in the Holocaust.

In the early part of the twentieth century, social movements around the globe threatened the racial superiority many white nations believed they simply inherited. Scientific tests were created and performed to prove white superiority. The tests themselves were designed to favor whites, but the results encouraged instances of racial sterilization in America and Europe, where the Nazi movement began its process of extermination based on the idea of white—particularly Aryan or Germanic—racial superiority.

## RACISM AND AMERICA: A CONFUSING RELATIONSHIP

America has a complicated relationship with race. Though the nation was created with ideals of freedom and equality, those rights were extended only to white men for more than a century. Born of English, French, and Spanish colonies, the United States was created by men who likely maintained European ideas of white superiority. Some of the nation's founders and earliest leaders were slaveholders, and until the conclusion of the Civil War, the nation's economy relied heavily on the slave trade and slave labor.

Though the Union soldiers and abolitionists defeated the Confederacy—which had the highest population of slaves—in the Civil War, racism in no way was defeated in the South. Rather, laws demanding racial segregation in all areas of life were enacted and harshly enforced. South-

America's first president, George Washington, owned slaves who lived in cabins like this one on his plantation in Mount Vernon, Virginia.

ern hostility and resentment for what many Southerners considered their "way of life" gave rise to hate groups such as the Ku Klux Klan, or KKK. For generations, groups like the KKK openly murdered, menaced, and harassed African Americans. The group still operates today and has grown in the twenty-first century.

Following the appalling events of World War II, international peace treaties and agreements brought an end to hostilities but not an end to racial disharmony. For instance, thousands of Japanese in America were held in internment camps during and after World War II because of Japan's wartime alliance with Italy and Germany.

# CHAPTER TWO

# A HISTORY OF RACISM

For centuries, imperialist European powers used notions of white superiority to justify their expansion in foreign countries and the oppression and enslavement of natives. The same racist notions eventually gave rise to fascist movements in Europe—such as Hitler's detainment and extermination of millions of Jews during World War II—and enslavement and segregation in the New World.

## SLAVERY, OPPRESSION, AND SEGREGATION: LAND OF THE UNFREE

America's short history is heavy with oppressive racial policies. The most well-known example is the enslavement of millions of Africans taken from their homes to provide free labor in colonial and postrevolutionary America. Other nonwhites and non-Christians—mostly Native Americans—were also enslaved when captured by European colonists.

In postrevolutionary America, the ideals of freedom and equality espoused by the writers of the constitution

Under the Nazi regime during World War II, Jewish people were detained in ghettos, like the Kutno Ghetto in Poland (pictured here). Most were sent to their deaths at concentration camps.

did not extend to the slaves who labored in their homes and fields—or to the thousands of slaves and freedmen who fought in the American Revolution. In fact, only white men had the right to vote in America for almost a hundred years. The founders clearly clung to some of their European roots, relying on traditionally European ideas of white superiority to justify slavery and refusing to acknowledge slaves as people. Many of the presidents between George Washington and Abraham Lincoln, the "Great Emancipator," were slaveholders.

Before slaves were liberated at the end of the Civil War (1865) with the enforcement of the Emancipation Proclamation, some four million slaves lived in the

This 1865 lithograph *Freedom for All, Both Black and White!* honors President Abraham Lincoln's Emancipation Proclamation.

Deep South alone. Slaves were usually subjected to harsh work and sparse living conditions. They faced severe punishment or death if they attempted escape or rebellion. Through forced migrations and the internal slave trade, many slave families were separated with little or no regard for their familial relationships.

Although the Emancipation Proclamation freed the slaves, Jim Crow laws kept African Americans living in the Southern states separate from whites in all aspects of public life. Public facilities and schools were segregated. Employment and economic disadvantages kept most African Americans impoverished. The Fifteenth Amendment, ratified in 1870, gave all men, regardless of color, the right to vote; however, Southern African Americans didn't fully realize their right to vote for another hundred years. Prohibitive measures like poll taxes and literacy tests kept African

Americans from fully participating in democracy until passage of the Voting Rights Act of 1965.

The 1960s provided the backdrop for the civil rights movement, in which minorities fought for basic rights still largely unrealized—even a hundred years after the Civil War. In 1961, President John F. Kennedy issued an executive order for affirmative action, which focused on fairness and equality in federal employment practices.

The Civil Rights Act of 1964 provided a legal basis for modern civil rights, particularly voting rights and segregation. The act gave birth to additional measures protecting minorities in America, such as the Equal Employment Opportunity Commission (EEOC), which protects minorities from discrimination in employment, housing, and education.

Despite legislation and policies in place to aid diversity in communities and in the job market, minorities still experience fewer advantages than their white peers. Jim Crow policies restricted African Americans from housing markets, schools, and employment opportunities. As a result, fewer African Americans have the means to grow wealth through gainful, professional employment attained from education, skilled training, or networking; without the financial means needed to own property, home ownership rates remain lower among African Americans and other minorities. This prevents them from moving to more desirable neighborhoods or school districts, effectively locking them into a cycle of racism dating back to the oppressive eras of slavery and Jim Crow.

# WHY ARE PEOPLE RACIST?

Unlike race itself, racism is not an innate trait in humans. Though members of the same family may share racist views, racism is not inherited from one generation to the next; rather, it's socialized.

A New York University study found that white male study participants, upon seeing a fleeting photo of an African American man, registered a spike of activity in the amygdala—the part of the brain associated with fear responses. Another study conducted by a neurosurgeon found that white study participants, upon seeing images of white faces, registered activity in the part of the brain responsible for facial recognition. The same applied to African American study participants who saw pictures

Protesters in New York City call for justice after the 2012 killing of Trayvon Martin, an unarmed seventeen-year-old who was shot by a member of the neighborhood watch in Florida.

of African Americans. Other-race (races not your own) images did not register as human faces like same-faces did. These findings are cause for concern; if a person of a certain race associates split-second contact with a person from another race as dangerous, the consequences could be deadly—as seen in cases like Mark Zimmerman and Trayvon Martin. When a person of one race does not immediately register a person of another race as human, socialized fearfulness is compounded by disregard for people of other races.

Generations of cultural messages about other races from family, experience, the media, and other avenues of cultural conditioning have shaped prejudice; humans constantly assign traits—bad or good—to people with certain physical characteristics. Humans will nurture and act on prejudices under duress or to gain approval from authority figures (think Nazi soldiers under Adolf Hitler's rule). These actions are typically what drive hate crimes.

The same research that found knee-jerk reactions to images of African Americans found that our prejudices can be minimized or abandoned by a combination of cultural beliefs and social circumstances. Essentially, we're capable of overwriting our hardwired prejudices. An Ohio State study discovered less amygdala activity in white research subjects who saw images of famous black people or when they were exposed to unfamiliar black faces for longer periods of time. This indicates that repeated and frequent exposure to other races could reduce the number of crimes between people of different races.

# MYTHS AND FACTS

**MYTH:** Affirmative action takes opportunities from white people.

**FACT:** Opposition to affirmative action persists among those who say it is an example of reverse racism. These opponents claim college and job opportunities favor minorities to meet affirmative action requirements instead of considering qualified whites. Affirmative action was a necessary measure to fix the underrepresentation of minorities in higher education and the work force. Though minorities are allegedly now considered equal, a FinAid student aid analysis found that white college students are 40 percent more likely to get private scholarships than minorities, and a National Bureau of Economic Research study on labor market discrimination shows white job applicants still receive about 50 percent more job opportunities than their African American peers.

**MYTH:** Civil rights legislation has effectively protected African Americans.

**FACT:** African Americans are still disproportionately affected by segregation and fewer opportunities than whites. Major cities have seen a rise in residential segregation and, therefore, a rise in school segregation; as African Americans and whites drift farther apart in cities, schools inevitably follow course. African Americans are also disproportionately incarcerated compared to whites.

**MYTH:** We live in a postracial society.

**FACT:** The 2008 election of Barack Obama, America's first black president, led many to speculate that we finally live in a postracial society. However, polling results showed significant polarization among whites, especially in the South. In the eight years Obama was president, racism experienced a renewed surge. The Tea Party, a political movement closely aligned with conservatism and the Republican Party, was comprised of primarily white members and fervently opposed—sometimes successfully—almost all of Obama's proposed policies. Per one law professor who wrote about white advantages in all areas of life, the income gap between African Americans and whites is higher than it's been in thirty years.

# CHAPTER THREE

# ARE WE REALLY STILL RACIST?

O n September 4, 1957, a group of teenagers were prohibited from entering Little Rock Central High on the first day of high school. An angry mob of students, parents, educators, and citizens, as well as the Arkansas National Guard, physically blocked the nine students. Called the Little Rock Nine, the African American students attempted to enroll at the high school before Arkansas was prepared or willing to desegregate schools. In the 1950s, most schools nationwide were still segregated. A 1954 landmark Supreme Court case called *Brown v. Board of Education* declared segregation in educational institutions illegal. The case allowed for local school districts to choose the best path forward to desegregate. Without an official time line from the court, desegregation moved slowly.

Then-governor Orval Faubus directly opposed the Little Rock Nine's integration into an all-white school. He had arranged the National Guard's presence to block the nine students from entering.

A few weeks later, President Dwight Eisenhower intervened and federal troops escorted the Little Rock Nine

In September 1957, nine black students in Little Rock attended a newly desegregated high school amidst violent threats. For their safety, they had to be escorted by a military detail.

into Central High on September 23. Even the presence of federal troops could not sway the minds of the indignant mob, who attacked the group and physically harmed some African American news reporters on the scene. A few hours into the school day, the mob became so unruly that Little Rock police ordered the nine students to leave through a back door and go home.

The group endured their first year at Central High amid threats and taunts; for the first few months, soldiers escorted the nine students in and out of the school building for their safety. When the military escort left for good, those nine students were left to fend for themselves.

The following year, Faubus retaliated against Eisenhower's federal intervention by shutting down all Little Rock schools for the 1958 to 1959 school year. Only two of the original nine students returned to Central High when Little Rock schools reopened by order of court rulings.

## POLITICAL RACISM: GOING BACKWARD

Terrence Roberts, one of the Little Rock Nine, says not much has changed since those controversial days at Central High more than half a century ago. Roberts, a psychologist and professor in California, has a unique psychosocial view on race relations, as both a key figure in the fight for integration and an expert in psychology. In early 2008—just months before Barack Obama was elected the country's first black president—Roberts told an interviewer that Americans are unwilling to admit they prefer a racially separated society. While he acknowledges that decisions like *Brown v. Board of Education* did much to change the law, Roberts points out nothing was done to change the socioeconomic conditions and habits that uphold segregation despite the laws prohibiting it. Three centuries of subhuman treatment of black people, Roberts says, has bled into modern social and political structures.

During his eight years as president, Obama—a Democrat and the first black president—seemed to be the catalyst for subversive racism in politics. The

The United States' first black president, Barack Obama, was elected in 2008 and reelected in 2012. Obama faced great opposition while in office, which many believe was racially motivated.

Tea Party, a far-right conservative political group, sprung up in reaction to Obama's election and immediately began voicing its opposition to almost all of Obama's proposed legislation. Legislation such as the Affordable Care Act (dubbed Obamacare by the media), aimed at providing equal access to health care for all Americans regardless of income, race, or gender, drew the ire of Republicans, conservatives, and far-right groups like the Tea Party. Some members of these groups became outwardly hostile to the president.

## RACISM: A NATIONAL INSTITUTION

African Americans account for about 13 percent of the total population in the United States. However, they account for almost half of all imprisoned people in this country. Racial profiling on the part of law enforcement officials has disproportionately affected African Americans. With on-the-scene deaths at the hands of police (such as Freddie Gray and Michael Brown, an unarmed eighteen-year-old African American shot by a policeman in 2014 after he allegedly robbed a St. Louis–area market), the world has watched as young black men are denied due process and die early deaths at the hands of authorities. Members of African American communities often report that police officers deployed to their neighborhoods typically have little knowledge of the community or culture. The split-second fearfulness and aggressiveness observed in white men exposed to African Americans could therefore inform the actions of police officers who don't attempt to overwrite their hardwired prejudices through education and exposure.

Criminal justice isn't the only social institution to feature discriminatory practices toward African Americans. Medical conditions that can be effectively managed when caught in the early stages, such as prostate cancer, high blood pressure, stroke, and diabetes, are commonly fatal to African Americans. The US government supports institutions that research health issues, but does not require researchers to include minorities in their research. Without a diverse group of subjects, medical research cannot accurately document the conditions as they apply to minority populations.

Education is another area of institutionalized racism. White citizens in affluent communities receive more property tax money for their public schools than poor minority areas. The separation in living conditions means children end up attending mostly segregated schools simply by virtue of where they live. Poor minorities face inherent racism in the housing market as well, as they're unlikely to have a credit history or savings for a down payment on a house. This keeps poor minorities trapped in the cycle of paying rent for what they do not own and prevents them from acquiring wealth and security.

According to a *Journal of Psychohistory* article about far-right movements, Obama was the most threatened president in history; the rate of threats against him was four times higher than it was for his Republican predecessor, George W. Bush. In 2013, Obama was the target of thirty death threats a day. The number of hate groups tracked by the Southern Poverty Law Center spiked during Obama's presidency, too, leading the center's president to comment that events such as the Charleston church shooting are obvious hate crimes, committed by people who feel threatened by the country's changing demographics and the increased prominence of African Americans in politics.

# HURRICANE KATRINA: A NATURAL AND SOCIAL DISASTER

In the last week of August 2005, the costliest natural disaster and one of the deadliest hurricanes in United States history pummeled Gulf Coast states. In addition to causing more than 1,200 deaths (estimates range from 1,245 to 1,836) and $108 billion in damages, Hurricane Katrina resulted in racial controversy as public outcry and debate grew over the inadequate federal response to the heavily African American city of New Orleans.

Sluggish government relief efforts during and after 2005's Hurricane Katrina disproportionately affected African Americans. Many were left homeless. Over 1,800 people died in the disaster.

As the world watched with horror, levees intended to protect New Orleans from flooding gave way. New Orleans residents who either wouldn't evacuate before the storm or couldn't because of a lack of resources (such as money or transportation) were literally washed away from their homes. Then-president George W. Bush has been criticized for missteps like negligence on the part of the Federal Emergency Management Agency (FEMA), which did not immediately respond to the disaster in New Orleans. To compound an already racially charged disaster, many media outlets portrayed African Americans as looters and rapists running rampant through the ravaged city. Local, state, and particularly federal authorities faced widespread public scrutiny and allegations of racially motivated neglect of the city. The social and economic toll of Hurricane Katrina has cast a shadow over the historic city of New Orleans, where damage to some buildings and infrastructure was never repaired. As those who had the resources and opportunity to relocate found homes outside the city or state (many of them moved to neighboring states like Texas), the city's remaining population was primarily poor African Americans without resources to rebuild homes and other structures. Through delayed responses from governmental agencies or lack of action altogether, many observers believe Hurricane Katrina exposed inherent racism in the United States—particularly in Southern states with a history of enslavement.

# CHAPTER FOUR

# VISIONS OF RACISM

In considering the struggle for equality, Americans might recall old photos taken during the civil rights movement, photos commonly shown to help tell the story of the movement's heroes.

## VISIONS OF BRAVERY: CIVIL RIGHTS PIONEERS

Envision a forty-two-year-old African American woman in Montgomery, Alabama, in a booking photo at the Montgomery Police Department on December 1, 1955. The woman is Rosa Parks. She's just been arrested for refusing to give up her seat in the "colored section" of the bus so white passengers could sit down. She was charged with disorderly conduct and had to pay a small fine. But what she ignited was much bigger: for almost a year, African Americans in Montgomery boycotted the bus service, putting a dent in the transit company's revenue. Montgomery repealed its law requiring segregation on public buses.

Five years later, four young African American men sit defiantly at a lunch counter in Greensboro, North Carolina, after they are refused service because of their skin color. It's February 1960. In refusing to get up from their seats, the young men helped spark a decade-long movement to challenge racial inequality in the South. Hundreds of students, civil rights organizations, faith-based congregations, and community members followed suit in a six-month protest of segregation.

Rosa Parks, seen here with Al Gore in 1999, was arrested in Alabama in December 1955 for refusing to give up her bus seat to a white man.

By July of that year, the lunch counter that started it all was desegregated.

Fast forward to 1963. Black-and-white photos from that year show some 250,000 people of all races following Martin Luther King Jr. in the March on Washington. The marchers were demanding national civil rights legislation and an end to racial injustice. In a rousing and momentous speech, King reminds marchers that a hundred years after the Civil War, African Americans are still not free. Segregation and discrimination continue to oppress them. King's profession of faith, delivered at the March on Washington, would continue to serve as a rallying cry for African Americans for generations to come: "I have a dream that one day this nation will rise up, live out the true meaning of its creed: 'We hold these truths to be self-evident, that all men are created equal.'"

Five years later, photos are finally printing in color. On April 3, 1968, King addresses a rally in Memphis, Tennessee. His flight to Memphis had been delayed by a bomb threat. When he finally reached the strikers, his speech addressed the fragility of life: "I would like to live a long life…But I'm not concerned about that now. I just want to do God's will. And He's allowed me to go up to the mountain. And I've looked over. And I've seen the promised land. I may not get there with you. But I want you to know tonight, that we, as a people, will get to the promised land."

At 6:01 p.m. the next day, King was fatally shot at his Memphis motel by James Earl Ray, a white man with a history of criminal activity. The civil rights community was devastated. The shooter's inconsistent admissions of guilt would eventually give rise to conspiracy theories alleging the US government engineered the assassination.

As the civil rights decade closes out, African Americans have lost their popular leader. King's death reminds them that despite their successes, they still must fear for their well-being. What's more, they're not sure they can count on their own government to keep them safe.

Half a century later, hateful supremacists like Dylann Roof prove that the African American community is still vulnerable.

## HOW RACISM LOOKS IN YOUR LIFE

Barack Obama's presidency probably seems normal to America's youth; after all, he was president for eight years. He may be the first president many adolescents and teenagers can clearly remember holding office. To the many civil rights activists who fought for equality on buses and at lunch counters, the ascendancy of an African American man to the highest office in the land would surely seem like a dream they may have never dared to imagine.

In the 1960s, families crowded around a television to watch shows and news; now, even if the news is on, chances are most people in the room are preoccupied with their cell phones. Vast amounts of information from around the globe are shared almost instantaneously and delivered to our mobile devices. Events that would have seemed momentous fifty years ago are now one of many headlines churned out in a weary, competitive twenty-four-hour news cycle. The news to which we have access is no longer relegated to the daily newspaper and the evening news. Now, information consumers can be selective about what news they consume.

White racists can get their "news" from any number of information brokers online. The internet is

For generations, Americans got their news from trusted journalists like Walter Cronkite. The advent of the internet has given rise to alternative media, some of which empowers racism.

the playground of radicals and extremists who successfully convince readers that they have authority over the information they share. The reality is much different. News and facts should be shared by vetted journalists with a history of unbiased reporting, otherwise "facts" are spun to reflect a website owner's or blogger's biased opinion. Racists like Roof will become emboldened by "facts" they consume from authoritative radicals online.

# CYBERRACISM

Most of us have heard of cyberbullying, where internet users take to social media sites, email, and other forms of online messaging to harass, shame, and intimidate their peers. Bullying has left the schoolyard and moved to internet-based methods that reach a large audience and further humiliate their victims. As one of the most severe forms of bullying (consider the daily harassment of the Little Rock Nine, years before the internet was a household commodity), racism has its hooks in cyberspace. Cyberracism can include racist websites, images, blogs, videos and racist comments, images and language sent via text, and internal messaging on networking sites. Essentially, any racism transmitted through electronic means with the goal of causing harm or distress to its target is cyberracism. Due to the nature of rapidly developing technologies, areas once considered private spaces are now public. Using internet features such as location identification, social networking sites, and online maps, cyberbullies can zero in on targets and make racist comments transmitted to thousands of people within seconds.

The increased use and accessibility of technology has given everyone the potential to self-publish their thoughts online. Many websites containing information that's factually incorrect have popped up. Some web content is developed specifically with racial motivations.

*(continued on the next page)*

*(continued from the previous page)*

Cyberracism makes use of communication technologies to repeatedly attack targets with hostile behavior. Because anything posted online can never truly be erased—copies exist on internet archives and potentially on individual hard drives or disks—cyberracism can have a prolonged impact on victims, including social, psychological, physical, and academic difficulties. Because the internet will retain some version of cyberracist activity associated with the name of the target of that racism, victims may never fully shed the burden of association with a particularly damaging form of cyberbullying.

If you're aware of cyberbullying, help put a stop to it by telling a teacher, parent, or guidance counselor. Ask them to intervene on behalf of the victim and the bully so that everyone involved can understand the full extent of the consequences of this particularly malicious form of bullying. Try to be sensitive in your own online activities: refrain from singling out people based on things they can't change, such as race, ethnicity, or sexual preference. Always approach online interactions with sensitivity and consider the lasting impacts a negative online presence can have. Once something is posted online, it's virtually there forever.

Protesters still gather to march, rally, and demand action from elected representatives the way civil rights–era Americans did. However, the nature of mobilization has changed with the widespread availability of the internet. For instance, the Black Lives

The Black Lives Matter movement arose in response to the deaths of African Americans at the hands of law enforcement.

Matter movement is largely centered online with some grassroots-level organizing up to local chapters across the country. Movements opposing white on black violence, particularly at the hands of police officers, are gaining momentum but have not yet reached the level of opposition as the civil rights and Black Power movements of the 1960s and 1970s.

# CHAPTER FIVE

# CONFRONTING RACISM

I dentifying racism as a current, prevalent social issue is the first step in confronting it. In this context, confrontation does not mean violence or aggression: it means taking responsibility for a situation in which the reader or someone he or she knows is involved in a racially charged situation. The many ways racism is carried out in the modern world, from hurtful Facebook comments or campaigns to the old ways of harassing someone in the hallways at school, can make following the thread of racist activity difficult. Taking extra care to be sensitive about what is said to or about someone else based on characteristics they cannot change is key.

But racist online communities aren't making it easy. According to some news reports, racial, homophobic and bigoted slurs are increasingly masked in code online to avoid censorship. Terms like Google, Skittle, and Yahoo have shown up as substitutes for insults describing African Americans, Muslims, and Mexicans. Figuring out the message could take a little detective work, but if it means a target of bullying or racist actions can be better protected, it's well worth the effort.

# IS HATE REALLY PROTECTED?

Because of federal laws and local policies that protect a person's right to free speech, schools, universities, municipalities, and other public and private institutions are left to decide what's appropriate and what's not—and whether policing what people say puts them in the position of possibly breaking the law.

The internet has given many racists a place to express hate speech and find others who share their views.

In early April 2017, the University of Central Florida had to face a challenge few institutions are prepared to take on: determining whether student messaging contained protected political speech or discriminatory speech that could lead to violence—or both.

In March 2017, a private Facebook group called UCF Underground listed an event targeting "dirty illegals." This came at a time when the country was in an uproar over President Donald Trump's attempts to detain or block access to travelers from a handful of Muslim countries and his promises to keep illegal immigrants from entering the United States.

In February 2017, protesters across the country rallied against Donald Trump's attempt to keep refugees out of the United States and impose a travel ban fo seven Muslim-majority countries.

Scheduled for April 2 at a restaurant close to the university campus, the "dirty illegals" event was aimed at teaching attendees how to identify illegal (undocumented) immigrants on social media and report them to the federal government.

Upon investigation, the event turned out to be a hoax.

## WHAT DO THE EXPERTS SAY?

Experts interviewed for an *Orlando Sentinel* story about the nature of the "dirty illegals" hoax warn that this kind of speech, when widely disseminated over social media forums, can incite violence or actual harass-ment. Like most private Facebook groups, UCF Underground provides a safe space for sharing ideologies. The *Sentinel* reports that many posts in the forum feature contro-versial opinions on racial and gender politics—two hot topics following the election of Donald Trump, who is internationally known for inflammatory speech. One post from January simply said, "Kill all Leftists," an inciting message geared toward eliminating Democrats and other liberal groups that oppose restrictive policies for immigrants, refugees, minorities, and women.

A symbol of the Confederacy, the Confederate flag's public presence in some areas of the South is still hotly debated.

What's more, UCF Underground contained posts associated with white nationalism. The same user who posted the "Leftist" message was tagged in a March photo where he was holding long-barreled guns in front of a Confederate flag.

Some countries and social networking sites like Facebook and YouTube have instituted policies prohibiting hate speech. However, free speech laws in the United States protect even hate groups. For decades, hate groups such as the KKK have been able to disseminate information about their beliefs to the public without recourse. While actions intended to harass or intimidate specific groups, such as the well-known KKK method of burning crosses on the lawns of African American homes or churches, are prohibited, the law has not caught up to the online equivalent of burning crosses. Administrators at the University of Central Florida can take no action against the UCF Underground conversation, no matter how much it may offend others or lead to real-world violence. When confronted with such a situation, the actions and words of fellow students who do not hold prejudicial views can go a long way: many racists were socialized to be that way by families or peer groups from their child-hood. Education about race and programs geared toward acceptance and compassion for other races and ethnicities should be a priority for any institution. Racism can be confronted or combated with messages of love and acceptance.

# 10 GREAT QUESTIONS TO ASK AN EXPERT

1. Where can I turn for trusted information about current events, especially those pertaining to race and immigration?
2. Should we do more to address racism in our community, and if so, what?
3. What does hate speech sound like?
4. What are some racial or ethnic concerns in our town, community, schools, and/or local government?
5. What are some of the most pressing racial concerns in the world right now, and how do you think they can be resolved?
6. What can I do alone or with my friends to combat racism?
7. What do you think could be done in public school curricula to better address our nation's history of racism and current issues?
8. How can my friends and I, and our school and community, promote cross-group contact so that we can interact with a diverse group of people?
9. How can we promote inclusiveness, compassion, and acceptance online?
10. How should we address spoken, written, or online hate speech when we hear it from our families, friends, and classmates?

# CHAPTER SIX

# WHEN RACISM GOES UNCHECKED

In photos documenting the event, the Little Rock Nine walk with their chins up, looking straight ahead, and don't show outward signs of fear. They were likely overwhelmed by nerves and feelings of anxiety. The angry mob greeting them at the school was loud, large in number, and openly espousing racist beliefs. The nine African American students had no way of knowing how or if they'd make it through the day, but they had to shove those thoughts away to claim what was rightly theirs.

## RACISM: A LEGACY OF STRESS AND TRAUMA

According to the American Psychological Association (APA), African Americans experience chronic stress because of pervasive racism and discrimination. Some African Americans may be so accustomed to daily encounters with racism, discrimination, and prejudice that they aren't even aware those biases

Although African Americans technically now have the same rights as white people, they still experience institutionalized racism in nearly all areas of their lives.

create a unique psychosocial condition. The stress is simply a part of their lives now. Per the APA, stress has serious physiological and psychological impacts and may be intertwined with other chronic diseases commonly seen in the African American population, such as hypertension.

Stress in African Americans may be obvious to them and to others; an African American job applicant may struggle with nagging insecurity about the racial views of a company's hiring manager. This worry may lead to physical reactions like sweating, an increased heart rate, and anxiety. Some African Americans who walk to work in a large city every day may have a subconscious concern for their safety based on current and past trends of violence toward African Americans. They may not actively acknowledge these safety concerns as persistent, but these thoughts may lurk in the back of their minds and cause emotional and physical strain. Because of the history of race relations in the United States, African Americans must consider social and political threats in ways most white people could not comprehend.

Even in our so-called postracial society, African Americans and other minority groups experience trauma because of racism. Trauma is a complex emotional response to an upsetting event; shock and denial are common first responses to a traumatic event, and delayed or long-term reactions include emotional highs and lows, flashbacks, and physical symptoms like nausea. Trauma can strain personal and professional relationships as the victim works through his or her emotions.

A trauma-inducing incident may happen directly to an individual or to a member of the community or culture with which they identify. As humans, we typically experience feelings of grief or anxiety when we hear about terrible events, no matter where they happened or to whom they happened. For instance, although the United States has a rocky relationship with Syria—specifically, Syria's leadership—many Americans were shocked and upset to learn Syrian President Bashar al-Assad killed at least seventy of his own people with poisonous gas on April 7, 2017. Distant observers

For years, refugees from parts of the Middle East have attempted to flee their home nations in search of refuge elsewhere. Many have died trying to get to safety.

usually feel sympathy for such horrifying events and sometimes even galvanize to send support of some kind to the affected population.

But imagine how Syrians feel after such an event. Fear for their safety would be of the utmost concern; anxiety about general violence would follow. The fear and anxiety following such a close call with death, or following the realization that your government does not share your concerns for the safety of yourself, your family, and your community, would be palpable.

Similarly, fears and anxiety for their safety would likely plague members of the African American

# EMPOWERING YOURSELF AND OTHERS

Deciding to act against racism is not always easy for victims of racism or even for people unaffected by the racism African Americans and other minorities experience. But participation from all concerned parties is necessary to fight against racism on all levels.

Young white people who want to get involved in combating racism should first take an inventory of their own social attitudes. While the desire to help end racism is a good indication of their respectful attitude toward people of other races or ethnicities, many people who deeply assess their hardwired attitudes are surprised by the number and variety of biases they harbor without conscious thought. A Harvard University endeavor, Project Implicit (implicit.harvard.edu), offers a free test for those who want to examine their attitudes.

For members of affected groups, finding support is key to overcoming stress, trauma, and anxiety. The APA suggests therapy and writing to help cope with current or past traumatic events. Finding support or community groups is always encouraged. Talking about traumatic events helps those affected lessen their individual emotional burden and brings them closer to others who can identify with certain experiences. The free exchange of ideas in a support group can help participants identify ways they can help not only themselves, but also affected family members, friends, and peers.

> **Help from all races, sexes, and cultures is need to help end racism; however, knowing yourself or knowing you're ready to take the step toward activism because you've dealt with your own personal experiences will make you a greater asset to the cause.**

community when police shootings of young, unarmed black men seem to occupy a frequent spot in the news. Houses of worship likely don't provide the sanctuary they once did following Roof's massacre in Charleston. This pervasive and unpredictable violence would cause intense feelings of mistrust, paranoia, and fear. Even seemingly minor incidents that involve a minority targeted for the color of their skin or their presumed religious beliefs may cause psychological harm in minorities or trigger flashbacks of previous trauma.

## BROADER IMPLICATIONS

The trauma of racially driven incidents doesn't stop with the target. By allowing events to repeat themselves, like the repeated incidents of young black men dying at the hands of police, the social and cultural impacts are enormous. Targeted groups like African Americans or other minorities begin to mistrust the system that's supposed to protect all citizens. Members of a targeted group may not feel comfortable calling the police to report any crime, big or small, because they aren't certain law enforcement is on their side. The repeated acquittals of law enforcement officials who fatally shoot African Americans and other minorities may, whether they are aware of it or not, assimilate the lack of consequences as justification for undue force or violence. While researchers and experts believe that overall, most police officers are not actively racist or prejudice and most don't want to use excessive or fatal violence, the split-second reactions they've been socialized to maintain for minorities overrides their sense of caution in tense situations. Hate groups experience little or no consequence for hate speech; they, too, would feel emboldened by the anonymity of the internet and the protections free speech laws afford them.

Accepting and honoring diversity is necessary for the world to move away from racially motivated crimes and hate speech.

Though antiracism action has always been an uphill battle, young people have the chance to change the story of racism starting this very day. Acknowledge that racism still plagues American society and look for ways to help. Collaborate with educators, parents, peers and advocacy groups to create a solid antiracism movement in your corner of the world. Let the leaders of today know that the voters of tomorrow will not let racism continue to end in death and the fracturing of our society.

**affirmative action** An action or policy favoring those who tend to suffer from discrimination, especially in relation to employment or education.

**bigotry** Intolerance of difference, especially toward members of a racial or ethnic group. It is usually accompanied by hatred of different groups.

**civil disobedience** The refusal to obey governmental demands or commands, especially as a nonviolent and usually collective means of forcing concessions from the government.

**civil rights** The nonpolitical rights of a citizen, specifically the rights of personal liberty guaranteed to United States citizens by the Thirteenth and Fourteenth Amendments to the US Constitution and by acts of the US Congress.

**cyber racism** A form of cyberbullying that makes use of information and communication technologies to deliberately transmit messaging that is racially offensive or racist in nature.

**discrimination** The unjust or prejudicial treatment of different categories of people or things, especially on the grounds of race or age.

**epithet** A word, phrase, or expression used as a term of abuse or contempt or to express hostility.

**eugenics** The study of or belief in the possibility of improving the qualities of the human species or a human population by discouraging reproduction among people with inheritable negative traits, and

encouraging reproduction among those with inheritable desirable traits.

**hate crime** A crime, usually violent, motivated by prejudice or intolerance toward an individual's national
origin, ethnicity, color, religion, gender, sexual orien-
tation, or disability.

**imperialism** The policy of extending the rule or authority of an empire or nation over foreign countries, or
of acquiring and holding colonies and dependen-
cies.

**minority** A group in society distinguished from, and
less dominant than, the more numerous majority; usually a racial, ethnic, religious, or social subdivision.

**nationality** The allegiance of an individual or group to
the state, typically characterized by common ori-
gins, traditions, and language.

**oppression** Unjust exercise of authority or power over
another group.

**postracial** A period of time or society in which racial
prejudice and discrimination no longer exist.

**prejudice** A preconceived judgment or opinion; an
adverse opinion or leaning formed without justification or without sufficient knowledge.

**racism** A belief that race is the primary determinant of
human traits and capacities and that racial differences
produce inherent superiority in a particular race.

**segregation** The institutional separation of an ethnic,
racial, religious, or other minority group.

**socialization** The process of familiarizing or training
members of a group for a particular social environ-
ment.

American Civil Liberties Union
125 Broad Street, 18th Floor
New York, NY 10004
(212) 549-2500
   Website: https://www.aclu.org
Twitter: @ACLU
Facebook: @aclu.nationwide
The American Civil Liberties Union is one of the foremost advocacy groups in the United States. It has worked to defend and preserve the individual rights and liberties guaranteed by the US Constitution. The ACLU has more than two million members, activists, and supporters in all fifty states, Puerto Rico, and Washington, DC, who safeguard rights.

National Association for the Advancement of Colored People (NAACP)
4805 Mount Hope Drive
Baltimore, MD 21215
(410) 580-5777
Website: http://www.naacp.org
Twitter: @NAACP
Facebook: @naacp
Instagram: @naacp
The NAACP has long worked to ensure the political, educational, social, and economic equality of rights of all persons and eliminate race-based discrimination. Founded in 1909, the NAACP is the nation's oldest

and most well-known grassroots-based civil rights organization. The organization was formed partially in response to the horrific practice of lynching.

Stand Against Racism
140 East Hanover Street
Trenton, NJ 08608
Website: http://standagainstracism.org
Twitter: @YWCAUSA
Facebook: @ywca.org
Instagram: @ywcausa
Stand Against Racism is a signature campaign of the Young Women's Club of America (YWCA) to build community among people who work for racial justice and raise awareness of the negative impacts of institutional and structural racism. The campaign is part of the group's overall national strategy to eliminate racism.

## WEBSITES

Because of the changing nature of internet links, Rosen Publishing has developed an online list of websites related to the subject of this book. This site is updated regularly. Please use this link to access the list:

http://www.rosenlinks.com/NTKL/Racism

# FOR FURTHER READING

Blood, Lisa. *Suspicious Nation: The Inside Story of the Trayvon Martin Injustice and Why We Continue to Repeat It.* Berkeley, CA: Counterpoint, 2014.

Bowman-Kruhm, Mary, and Claudine Wirths. *Coping with Discrimination and Prejudice.* New York, NY: Rosen Publishing Group, 2000.

Chang, Jeff. *We Gon' Be Alright: Notes on Race and Resegregation.* New York, NY: Macmillan/Picador, 2016.

Charles River Editors. *Hurricane Katrina: The Story of the Destructive Hurricane in American History.* CreateSpace Independent Publishing Platform, 2014.

Coates, Ta-Nehisi. *Between The World And Me.* New York, NY: Spiegel & Grau, 2015.

Dyson, Michael Eric. *The Black Presidency: Barack Obama and the Politics of Race in America.* New York: Houghton Mifflin Harcourt Publishing Company, 2016.

Fairbanks, Daniel J. *Everyone is African: How Science Explodes the Myth of Race.* Amherst, NY: Prometheus Books, 2015.

Fulton, Sybrina, and Tracy Martin. *Rest in Power: The Enduring Life of Trayvon Martin.* New York, NY: Spiegel & Grau, 2017.

Hayes, Chris. *A Colony in a Nation.* New York, NY: W. W. Norton & Company, 2017.

Krell, Bruce E. *Ferguson, MO: What Really Happened: A Systemic, Scientific Analysis.* North Charleston, SC: Shooters-Edge, Inc., 2015.

Martin, Rose Laura. *The Ku Klux Klan or Invisible Empire.* Los Angeles, CA: HardPress Publishing, 2013.

Miller, Jake. *Brown v. Board of Education of Topeka: Challenging School Segregation in the Supreme Court* (Library of the Civil Rights Movement). New York, NY: Rosen Publishing Group, 2004.

Miller, Jake. *The Montgomery Bus Boycott: Integrating Public Buses* (Library of the Civil Rights Movement). New York, NY: Rosen Publishing Group, 2004.

Miller, Jake. *The 1963 March on Washington: Speeches and Songs for Civil Rights* (Library of the Civil Rights Movement). New York, NY: Rosen Publishing Group, 2004.

Miller, Jake. *Sit-Ins and Freedom Rides: The Power of Nonviolent Resistance* (Library of the Civil Rights Movement). New York, NY: Rosen Publishing Group, 2004.

Phillips, Patrick. *Blood at the Root: A Racial Cleansing in America.* New York, NY: W. W. Norton & Company, 2016.

Roithmayr, Daria. *Reproducing Racism.* New York, NY: New York University Press, 2014.

Ryan, April. *The Presidency in Black and White.* Lanham, MD: Rowman & Littlefield, 2015.

Smith, Mychal Denzel. *Invisible Man, Got the Whole World Watching: A Young Black Man's Education.* New York, NY: Nation Books, 2016.

Alexander, Lisa Doris. "Brown v. Board of Education (Brown I)." Retrieved April 1, 2017. https://africanamerican.abc-clio.com.

Alexander, Lisa Doris. "Brown v. Board of Education (Brown I)." Retrieved April 1, 2017. https://africanamerican.abc-clio.com.

Bertrand, Marianne, and Sendhil Mullainathan. "Are Emily and Greg More Employable Than Lakisha and Jamal? A Field Experiment on Labor Market Discrimination." National Bureau of Economic Research, July 2003.

Dingfelder, Sadie F. "Not Much Has Changed." American Psychological Association Monitor, Vol. 39, No. 1, January 2008.

Ellis, Blake A. "Little Rock Nine." The American Mosaic: The African American Experience, ABC-CLIO, 2017. http://africanamerican.abc-clio.com/Search/Display/1477400.

"15th Amendment to the U.S. Constitution," Library of Congress Primary Documents in American History. Retrieved April 12, 2017. https://www.loc.gov/rr/program/bib/ourdocs/15thamendment.html.

"History of Hate: Crimes Against Sikhs Since 9/11." Huffington Post, August 7, 2012, http://www.huffingtonpost.com/2012/08/07/history-of-hate-crimes-against-sikhs-since- 911_n_1751841.html.

Kantrowitz, Mark. "The Distribution of Grants and Scholarships by Race." FinAid!, September 2, 2011. http://www.finaid.org/scholarships/20110902racescholarships.pdf.

Lotto, David. "The South Has Risen Again: Thoughts on the Tea Party and the Recent Rise of Right-Wing

Racists." *Journal of Psychohistory,* Volume 43 (3), Winter 2016.

Marsh, Jason, Rodolfo Mendoza-Denton, and Jeremy Adam Smith. *Are We Born Racist?*, Boston, MA: Beacon Press, 2010.

McGuire, William, and Leslie Wheeler. "Rosa Parks." The American Mosaic: The African American Experience, ABC-CLIO, 2017. http://africanamerican.abc-clio.com/Search/Display/1504683.

Roithmayr, Daria. *Reproducing Racism.* New York, NY: New York University Press, 2014.

Sack, Kevin. "Already Facing Death, Dylann Roof Cuts Deal for Added Life Term." *New York Times*, March 31, 2017. https://www.nytimes.com/2017/03/31/us/dylann-roof-charleston-ame-church-guilty-plea.html.

Smith, Wilson. "Unrest in Ferguson, Missouri." The American Mosaic: The African American Experience, ABC-CLIO, 2017. africanamerican.abc-clio.com/Search/Display/1960559.

"*Trauma.*" *Psychology Topics, the American Psychological Association*, http://www.apa.org/topics/trauma/index.aspx.

Woodworth, Steven. "American Civil War." World History: The Modern Era, ABC-CLIO, 2017. http://worldhistory.abc-clio.com/Search/Display/309429.

## A

affirmative action, 19, 22
Affordable Care Act, 27
African Americans, 5, 9, 18–22,
    28–29, 31–35, 39–40, 44,
    46–49, 51

## B

Black Lives Matter, 5, 38–39
*Brown v. Board of Education*,
    24, 26
bullying, 37–38, 40

## C

Charleston church shooting, 29
civil rights, 4, 38–39
Civil Rights Act, 19
civil rights movement, 7, 19, 32
Civil War, 7, 14, 17, 19, 33
Confederacy, 4, 14, 43
cyberbullying, 37–38

## D

discrimination, 19, 34, 46

## E

education, 6, 19, 22, 24, 26,
    28–29, 44

ethnicity, 7–8, 10, 38, 44, 50
eugenics, 13

## F

free speech laws, 44, 52

## G

Gray, Freddie, 5, 28

## H

hate crimes, 29
hate groups, 6, 15, 29, 44
hate speech, 41, 44, 52

## I

immigrants, 9–10, 42–43

## J

Jim Crow, 18–19

## K

Katrina, Hurricane, 30–31
King, Martin Luther, Jr., 33, 34
Ku Klux Klan, 15

## L

Lincoln, Abraham, 17

## ABOUT THE AUTHOR

Angie Timmons is a writer who studied journalism and sociology at Texas Tech University. After working as a reporter and editor for newspapers in Central Texas, she has worked in health information and as a technical writer and content manager for software and communications companies in the Dallas–Fort Worth area since 2011. She has written two other titles for Rosen: *The Nanjing Massacre* (Bearing Witness) and *How to Create Digital Portfolios to Show What You Know*. She lives in a Dallas suburb with her husband, Jason, and their three cats.

## PHOTO CREDITS

Cover oliveromg/Shutterstock.com; back cover Photo by Marianna armata/Moment/Getty Images; p. 5 Anadolu Agency/Getty Images; pp. 7, 16, 24, 32, 40, 46 Lucky Business/Shutterstock.com; p. 8 Keystone-France/Gamma-Keystone/Getty Images; p. 11 © Nancy Carter/North Wind Picture Archives; p. 14 John Greim/Loop Images/Corbis Documentary/Getty Images; p. 17 Hugo Jaeger/The LIFE Picture Collection/Getty Images; p. 18 Fine Art/Corbis Historical/Getty Images; p. 20 Allison Joyce/Getty Images; p. 25 A. Y. Owen/The LIFE Picture Collection/Getty Images; p. 27 Chip Somodevilla/Getty Images; p. 30 Mario Tarna/Getty Images; p. 33 Paul Sancya/AFP/Getty Images; p. 36 CBS Photo Archive/CBS/Getty Images; p. 39 Kena Betancur/Getty Images; p. 41 vm/E+/Getty Images; p. 42 Scott Olson/Getty Images; p. 43 Sean Rayford/Getty Images; p. 47 Brooke Fasani Auchincioss/The Image Bank/Getty Images; p. 49 Paula Bronstein/Getty Images; p. 52 PeopleImages/DigitalVision/Getty Images.

Design: Michael Moy; Layout: Tahara Anderson;
Photo Researcher: Nicole Baker